Worship BAND PLAY-ALONG

DRUMSET EDITION   *Volume 4*

He Is Exalted

T0081537

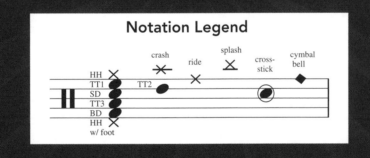

Recorded and produced by Jim Reith at BeatHouse Music, Milwaukee, WI

Lead Vocals by Tonia Emrich and Jim Reith
Background Vocals by Jim Reith and Joy Palisoc Bach
Guitar by Jim Reith
Bass by Chris Kringel
Keyboard by Kurt Cowling
Drums by Del Bennett

ISBN 978-1-4234-1730-9

HAL•LEONARD® CORPORATION

7777 W. BLUEMOUND RD. P.O. BOX 13819 MILWAUKEE, WI 53213

Beautiful One

Words and Music by Tim Hughes

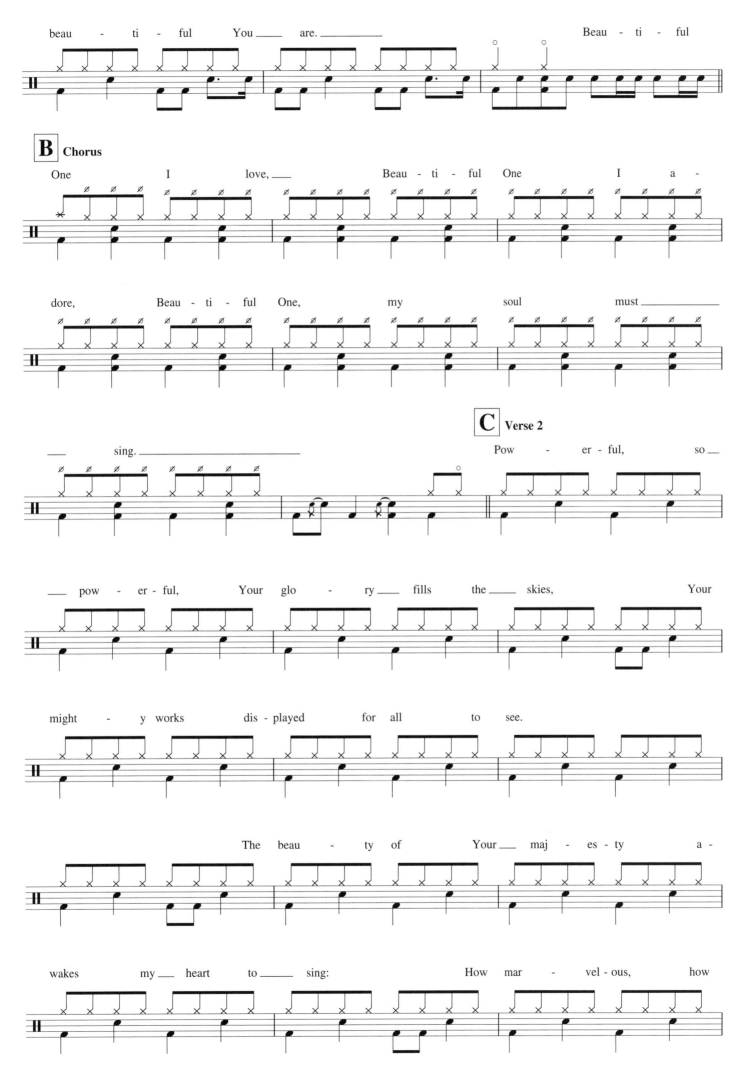

Bridge
You o - pened my eyes to Your won - ders a - new, You cap -
- tured my heart with this love, 'cause noth - ing on earth is as beau -
- ti - ful as You. Beau - ti - ful
F
Chorus
One I love, Beau - ti - ful One I a -
dore, Beau - ti - ful One, my soul must
sing.
Chorus
Beau - ti - ful One I love,
Beau - ti - ful One I a - dore, Beau - ti - ful
One, my soul must sing.

God of All

Words and Music by Twila Paris

He Is Exalted

Words and Music by Twila Paris

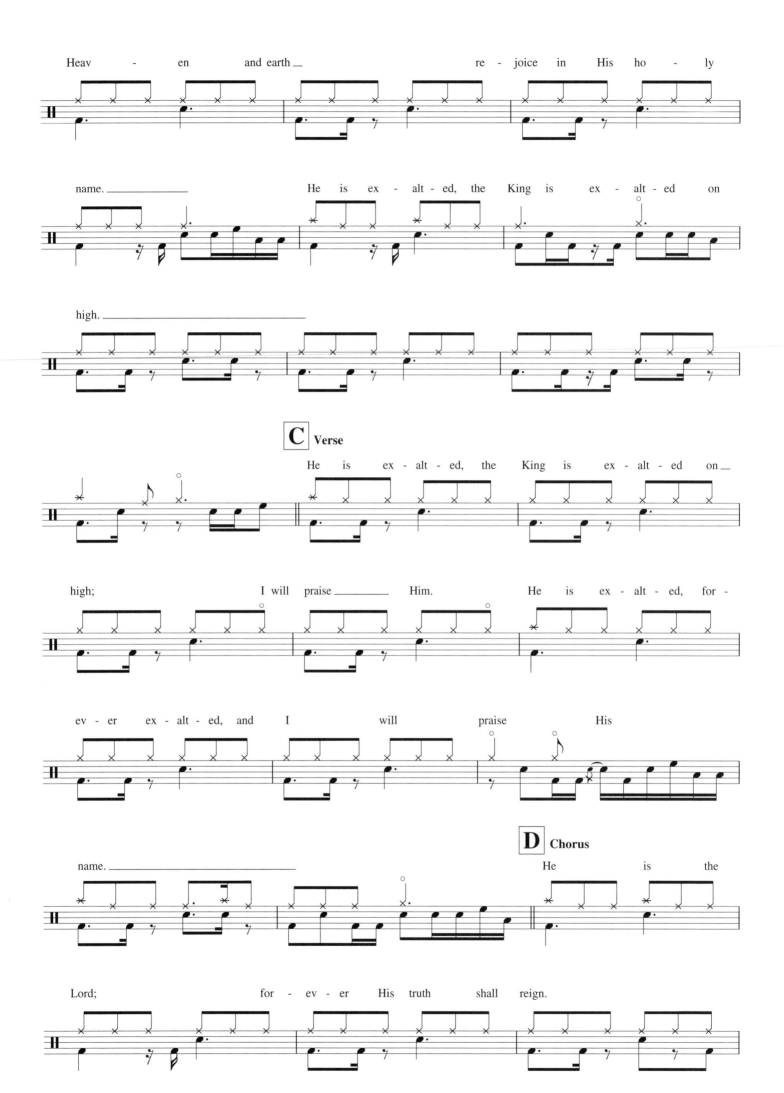

In Christ Alone

Words and Music by Keith Getty and Stuart Townend

TRACKS
7/8

With conviction (♩ = 78)

Intro

(Piano)

A **Verse 1**

In Christ a - lone my hope is found. He is my

light, my strength, my song. This Cor - ner - stone, this sol - id ground, firm through the

fierc - est drought and storm. What heights of love, what depths of

peace, when fears are stilled, when striv - ings cease. My Com - fort - er, my All in

All, here in the love of Christ I stand. In Christ a-

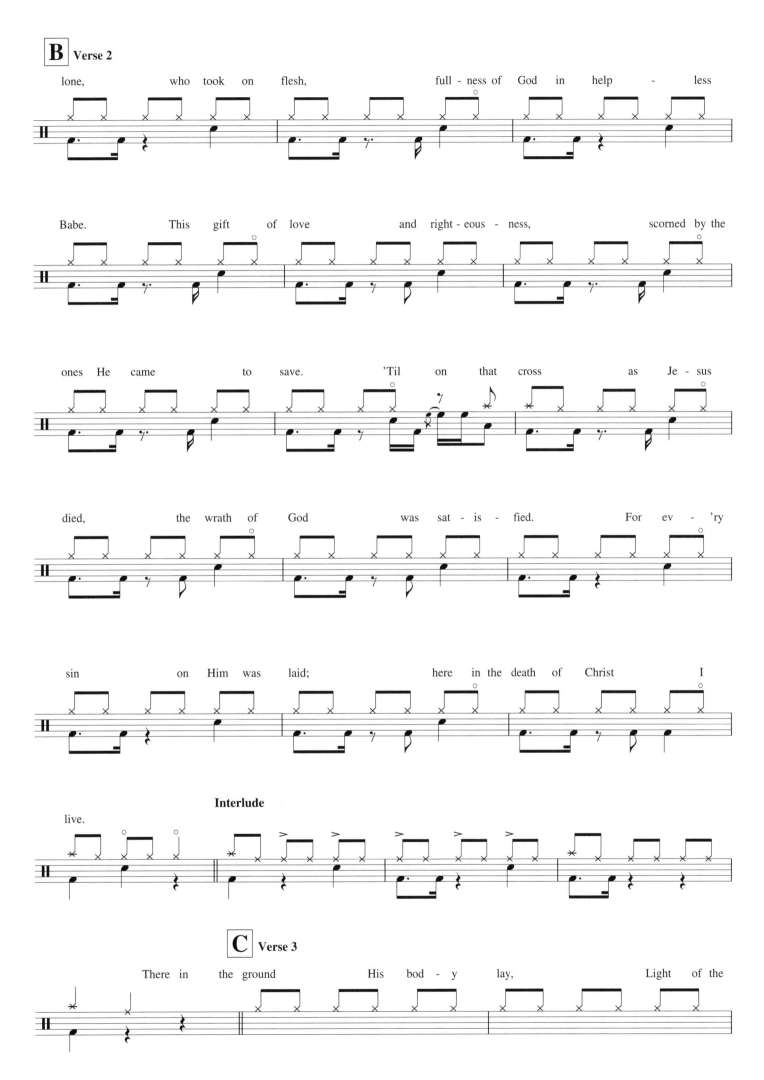

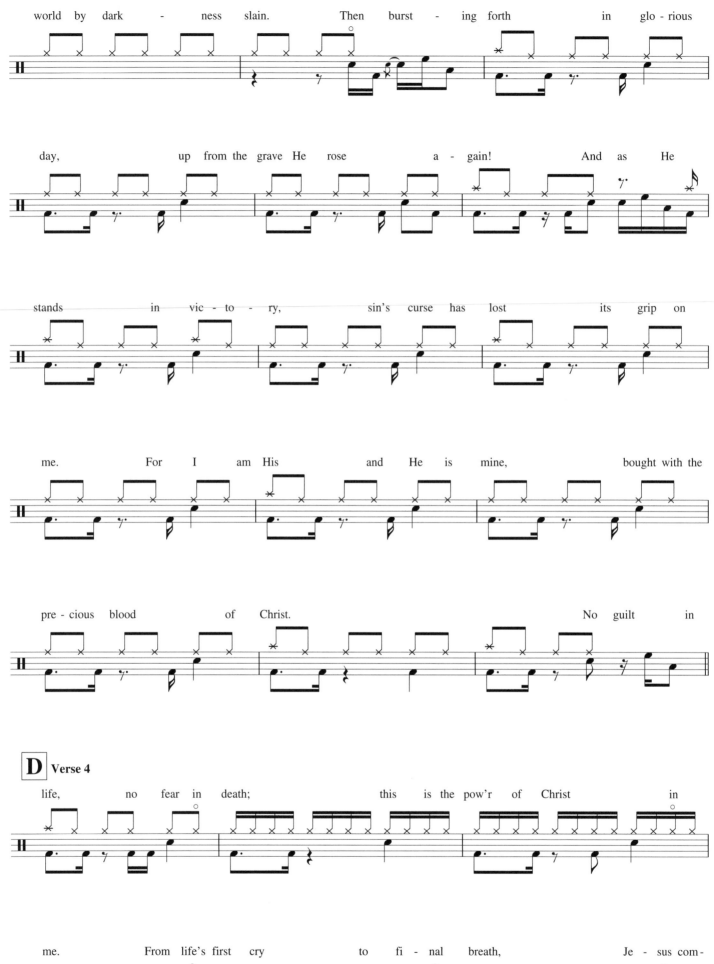

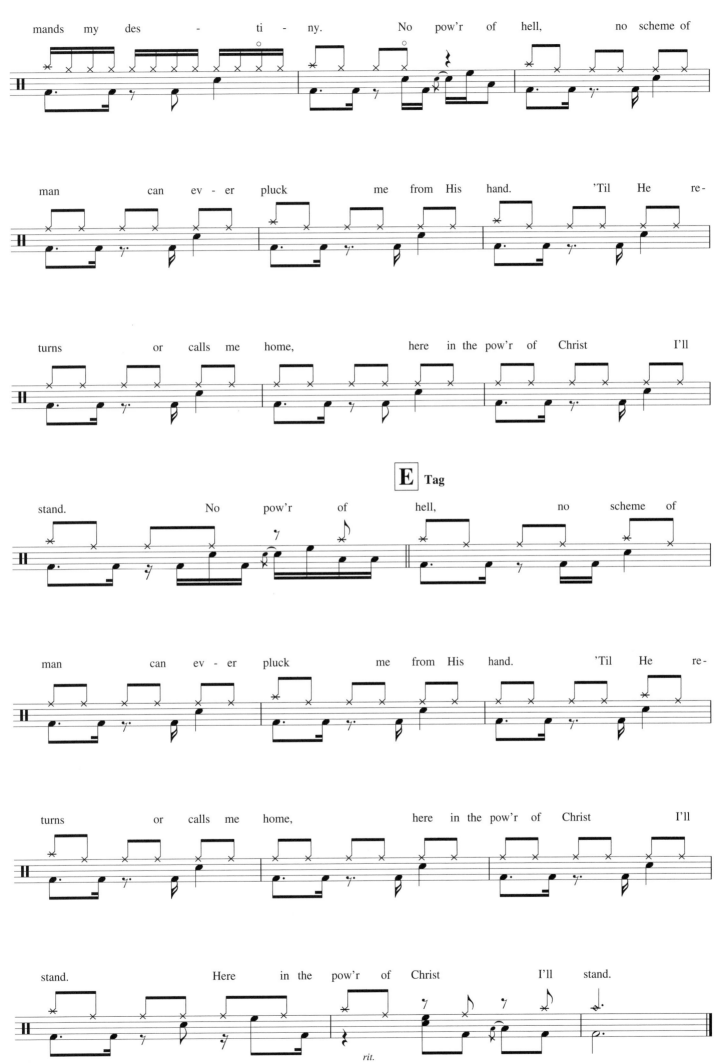

Lord Most High

Words and Music by Don Harris and Gary Sadler

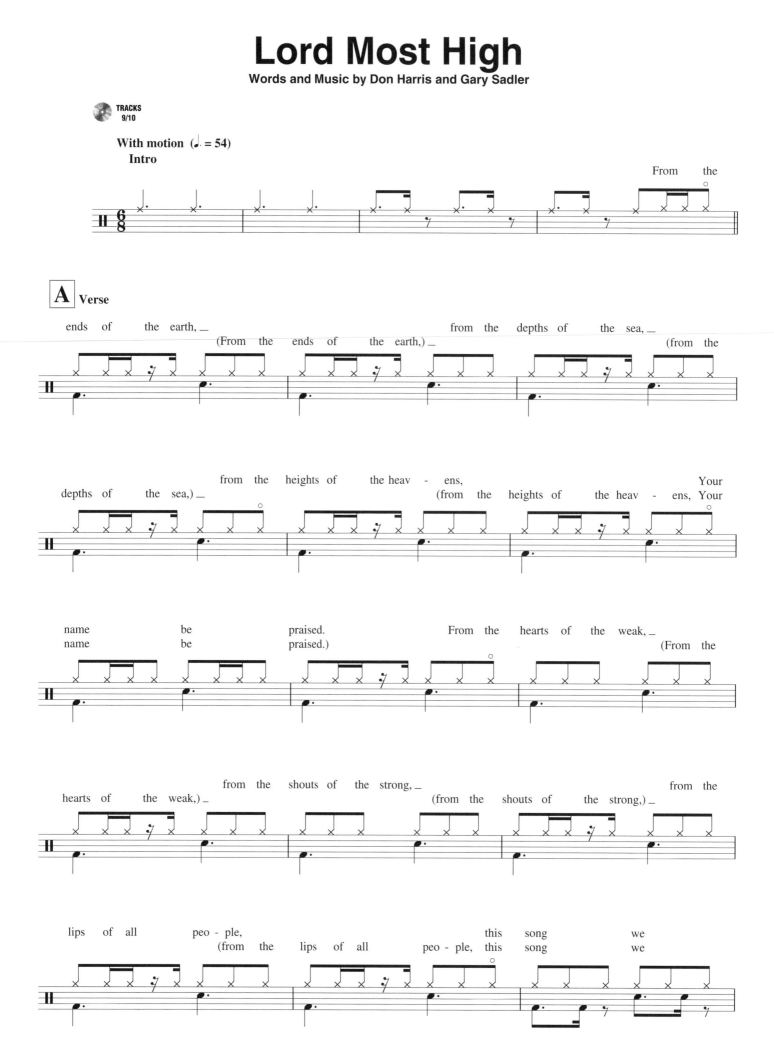

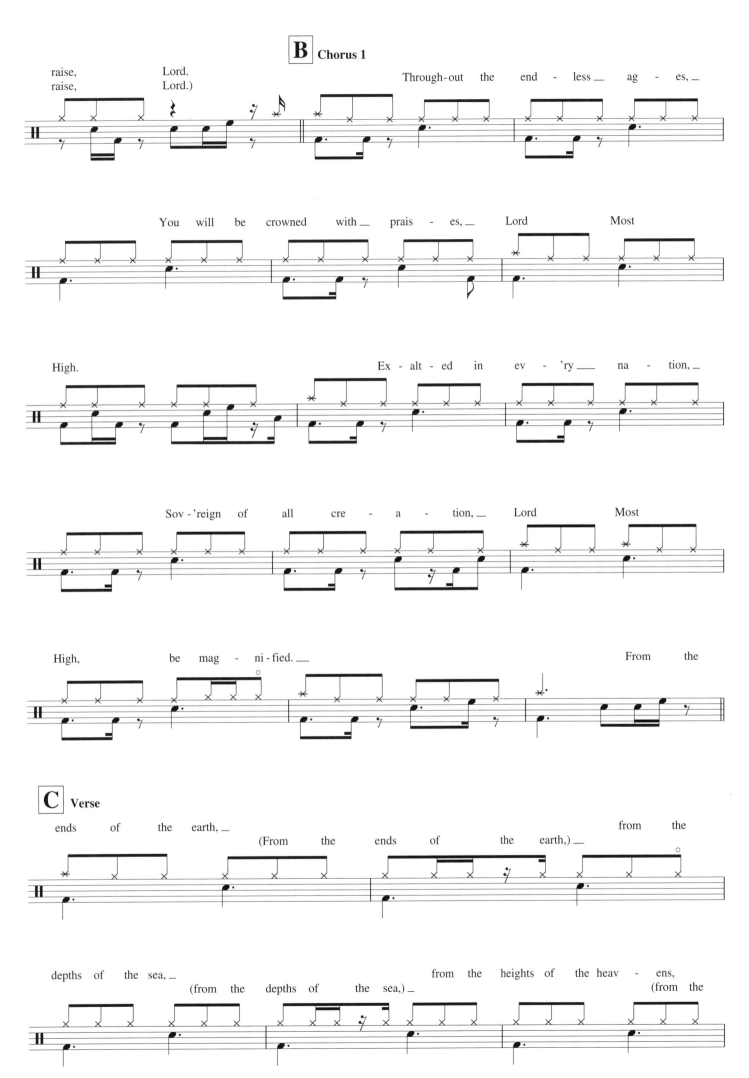

D Chorus 2

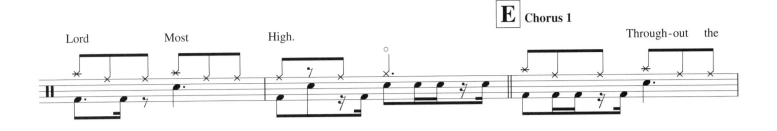

Lord   Most   High.   Through-out   the

E   Chorus 1

end - less __ ag - es, __   You will   be   crowned   with   prais - es, __

Lord   Most   High.   Ex - alt - ed   in

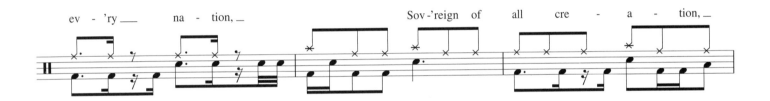

ev - 'ry __ na - tion, __   Sov-'reign of   all   cre - a - tion, __

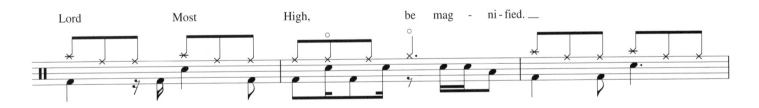

Lord   Most   High,   be   mag - ni - fied. __

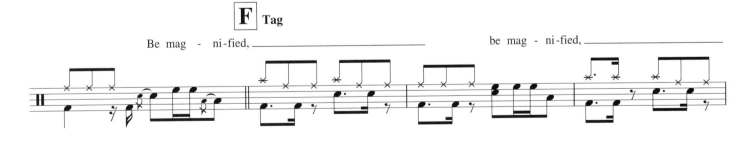

F   Tag

Be mag - ni - fied, _____   be mag - ni - fied, _____

Lord   be mag - ni - fied, _____   be mag - ni - fied.

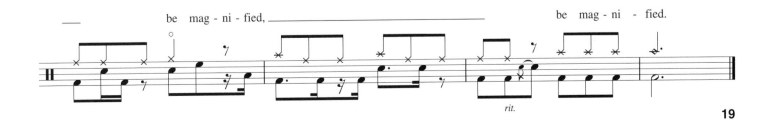

rit.

Lord, Reign in Me

Words and Music by Brenton Brown

Interlude

C **Verse 2**

D **Chorus**

21

We Want to See Jesus Lifted High

Words and Music by Doug Horley

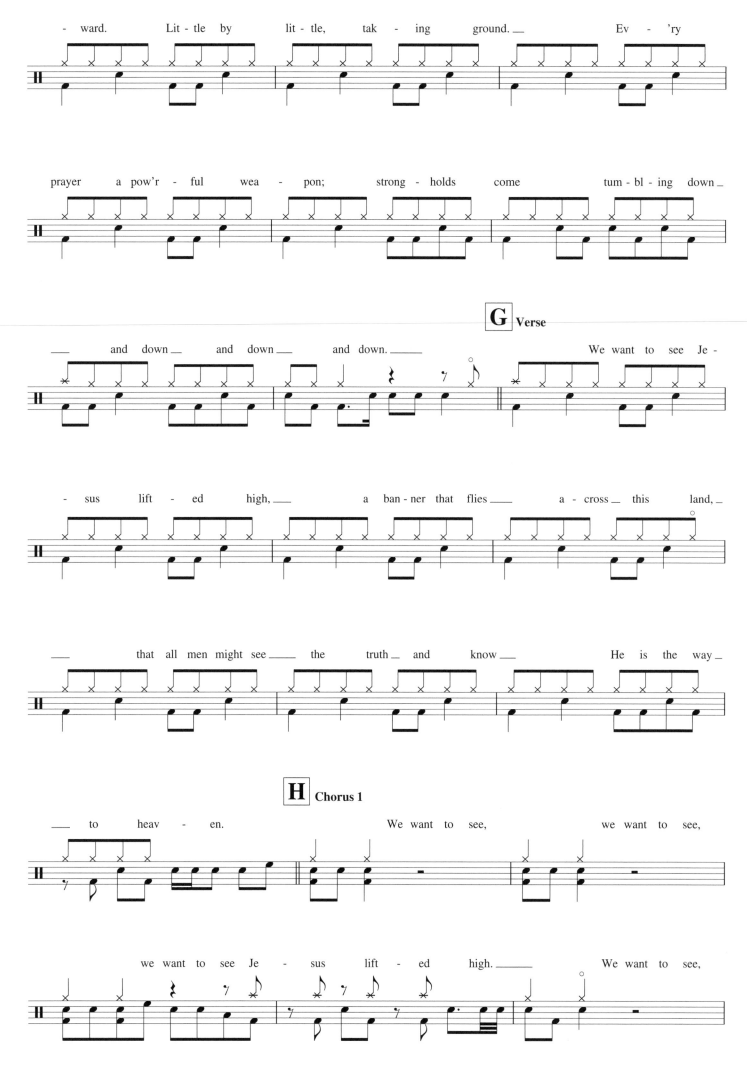

I Chorus 2

J Outro

Worthy Is the Lamb

Words and Music by Darlene Zschech

give - ness and __ em - brace. __   Wor - thy is ___ the Lamb, __

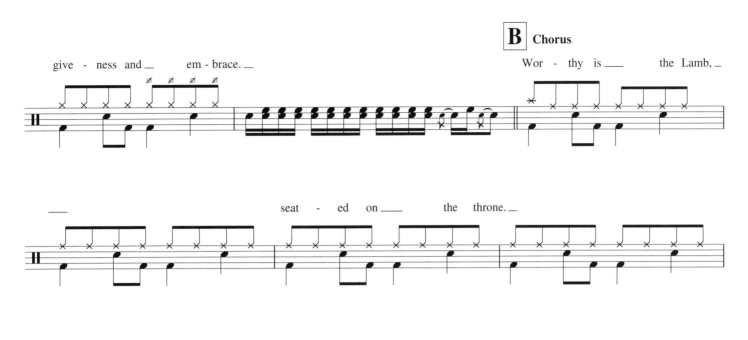

__ seat - ed on ___ the throne. __

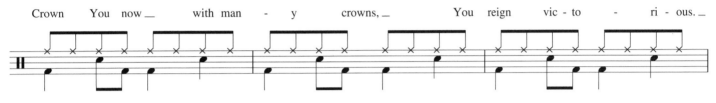

Crown You now __ with man - y crowns, __   You reign vic - to - ri - ous. __

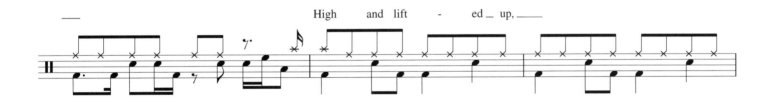

__ High and lift - ed _ up, ____

Je - sus, Son __ of God. __   The Treas - ure of heav - en cru -

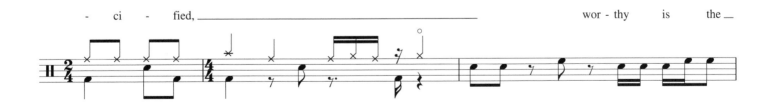

- ci - fied, _____ wor - thy is the __

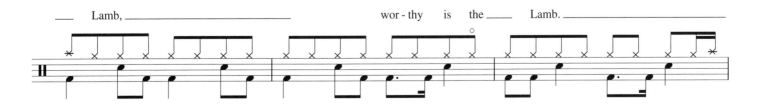

__ Lamb, _____ wor - thy is the ___ Lamb. _____

Verse

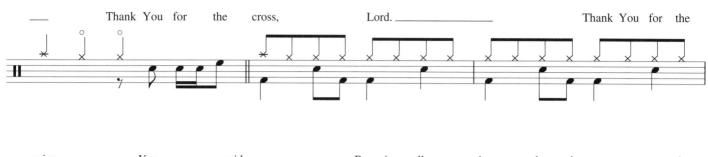

Thank You for the cross, Lord. _____ Thank You for the

price You paid. ___ Bear -ing all my sin and ___ shame, ___ in

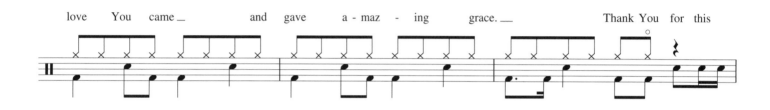

love You came ___ and gave a - maz - ing grace. ___ Thank You for this

love, Lord. _____ Thank You for the nail - pierced hands. ___

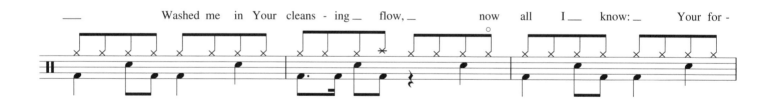

___ Washed me in Your cleans - ing ___ flow, ___ now all I ___ know: ___ Your for -

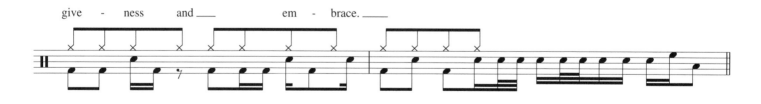

give - ness and ____ em - brace. ____

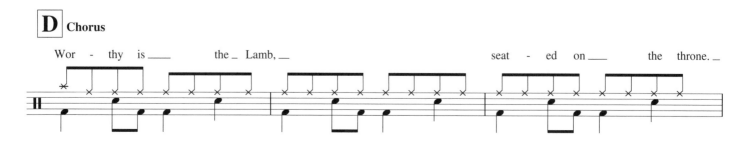

D **Chorus**

Wor - thy is ____ the _ Lamb, ___ seat - ed on ___ the throne. _

BEAUTIFUL ONE

TIM HUGHES

Key of **D Major, 4/4**

INTRO:

G A Bm7 A

G A D

VERSE 1:

G   A   D/F♯
Wonderful, so wonderful is Your unfailing love

      G   A   Bm7
Your cross has spoken mercy over me

   G   A   D/F♯
No eye has seen, no ear has heard, no heart could fully know

     G   A   D
How glorious, how beautiful You are

CHORUS:

         G   A   G   A
Beautiful One I love, Beautiful One I adore

        G   A   D
Beautiful One, my soul must sing

VERSE 2:

G   A   D/F♯
Powerful, so powerful, Your glory fills the skies

      G   A   Bm7
Your mighty works displayed for all to see

     G   A   D/F♯
The beauty of Your majesty awakes my heart to sing:

    G   A   D
How marvelous, how wonderful You are

(REPEAT CHORUS 2X)

BRIDGE (2X):

     G   A
You opened my eyes to Your wonders anew

     G   A
You captured my heart with this love

       G   A   D
'Cause nothing on earth is as beautiful as You

(REPEAT CHORUS 2X)

GOD OF ALL

TWILA PARIS

Key of **E Major, 4/4**

INTRO (2X):

E   B/D♯   C♯m7   Bsus

VERSE:

E   B/D♯
God of all, we come to praise You

   A/C♯   Bsus
We lift Your name on high in all the earth

E   B/D♯
God of all, we come to praise You

   A/C♯   Bsus
We lift Your name on high in all the earth

CHORUS 1:

     E/G♯ Bsus   B   E/G♯ Bsus   B
God of glo - ry,   God of maj - es - ty

     E/G♯ Bsus E/G♯   A Bsus
God of mer - cy, we lift Your name on high

     E A Bsus   E A Bsus
God of all,   God of all

(REPEAT VERSE)

CHORUS 2:

     E/G♯   Bsus   B   E/G♯   Bsus   B
God of ho - li - ness,   God of righteousness

     E/G♯ Bsus E/G♯   A Bsus
God of heav - en, we lift Your name on high

     E/G♯ Bsus   B   E/G♯ Bsus   B
God of glo - ry,   God of maj - es - ty

     E/G♯ Bsus E/G♯   A Bsus
God of mer - cy, we lift Your name on high

TAG:

     E   A   Bsus
God of all (We lift Your name on high, we lift Your name on high) **REPEAT 4X**

     E (hold)
God of all

HE IS EXALTED
TWILA PARIS

Key of **F Major, 6/8**

INTRO:

F   C/F   B♭/F

F   C/F   B♭/F

VERSE:

F   F/A   B♭
He is exalted, the King is exalted on high

     B♭/D   C/E
I will praise Him

F   F/A
He is exalted, forever exalted

   B♭ C/B♭ B♭/C   C Dsus   D/C
And I   will   praise His name

CHORUS:

Gm Dm/F   C/E C
He   is the Lord

    F   Am7   B♭   F/A
Forever His truth shall reign

Gm Dm/F   C/E C
Heav - en and earth

    F   Am7 B♭   F/A
Rejoice in His holy name

Gm   Gm/F   E♭   B♭/C   (F)
He is exalted, the King is exalted on high

(REPEAT INTRO)

(REPEAT VERSE)

(REPEAT CHORUS 2X)

TAG:

C/D D/F♯ Gm   Gm/F   E♭   B♭/C   F (hold)
            He is exalted, the King is exalted on high

IN CHRIST ALONE

KEITH GETTY and STUART TOWNEND

TRACKS
7/8

Key of **D Major**, 3/4

INTRO (2X):

Am7   Em7   D Dsus D

VERSE 1:

  G/D   D   G   A
In Christ alone my hope is found

D/F♯   G   Em7 Asus   D
He is my light, my strength,   my song

     G/D   D   G   A
This Cornerstone, this solid ground

D/F♯   G   Em7 Asus   D
Firm through the fiercest drought and storm

     D/F♯   G   D/F♯   A
What heights of love, what depths of peace

     D/F♯   G   Bm7   A
When fears are stilled when strivings cease

  G   D   G   A
My Comforter, my All in All

D/F♯   G   Em7 Asus   D
Here in the love of Christ   I stand

(Dsus D)

VERSE 2:

In Christ alone, who took on flesh
Fullness of God in helpless Babe
This gift of love and righteousness
Scorned by the ones He came to save
'Til on that cross as Jesus died
The wrath of God was satisfied
For ev'ry sin on Him was laid
Here in the death of Christ I live

INTERLUDE:

Am7   Em7   D Dsus D

VERSE 3:

There in the ground His body lay
Light of the world by darkness slain
Then bursting forth in glorious day
Up from the grave He rose again!
And as He stands in victory
Sin's curse has lost its grip on me
For I am His and He is mine
Bought with the precious blood of Christ

(Dsus D)

VERSE 4:

No guilt in life, no fear in death
This is the pow'r of Christ in me
From life's first cry to final breath
Jesus commands my destiny
No pow'r of hell, no scheme of man
Can ever pluck me from His hand
'Til He returns or calls me home
Here in the pow'r of Christ I'll stand

TAG:

    D/F♯   G   D/F♯   A
No pow'r of hell, no scheme of man

    D/F♯ G   Bm7   A
Can ever pluck me from His hand

   G   D   G   A
'Til He returns or calls me home

D/F♯   G   Em7 Asus   D
Here in the pow'r of Christ   I'll stand

D/F♯   G   Em7 Asus   D (hold)
Here in the pow'r of Christ   I'll stand

LORD MOST HIGH

DON HARRIS and GARY SADLER

Key of **E Major**, 6/8

INTRO (2X):

E Esus E Esus2

VERSE:

            E   *Echo:* Esus   E
From the ends of the earth (from the ends of the earth)
           B   Bsus   B
From the depths of the sea (from the depths of the sea)
       C♯m7
From the heights of the heavens (from the heights of the heavens)
    A E/A A
Your name be praised
            E   Esus   E
From the hearts of the weak (from the hearts of the weak)
           B   Bsus   B
From the shouts of the strong (from the shouts of the strong)
       C♯m7
From the lips of all people (from the lips of all people)
    A E/A A   B
This song we raise, Lord

CHORUS 1:

E E/G♯   A   B
Throughout the endless ages
E E/G♯   A   B
You will be crowned with praises
C♯m7 A Bsus B
Lord Most High
E E/G♯   A   B
Exalted in ev'ry nation
E E/G♯   A   B
Sov'reign of all creation
C♯m7 A   B E/G♯   A
Lord Most High, be magnified

(REPEAT VERSE)

CHORUS 2:

E E/G♯   A   B
Throughout the endless ages
E E/G♯   A   B
You will be crowned with praises
C♯m7 A Bsus B
Lord Most High
E E/G♯   A   B
Exalted in ev'ry nation
E E/G♯   A   B
Sov'reign of all creation
C♯m7 A Bsus B
Lord Most High

(REPEAT CHORUS 1)

TAG:

B   E E/G♯ A
     Be magnified   **REPEAT 2X**
B   E (hold)
Be magnified

LORD, REIGN IN ME

BRENTON BROWN

 TRACKS
11/12

Key of **G Major, 4/4**

INTRO:

G D C G D C

VERSE 1:

G   D   C   D
    Over all the earth, You reign on high

G   D   C   D
    Ev'ry mountain stream, ev'ry sunset sky

Em7   D   C   D   Am7
    But my one request, Lord, my only aim

        C   D
Is that You'd reign in me again

CHORUS:

G   D   C   D
    Lord, reign in me, reign in Your pow'r

G   D   C   D
    Over all my dreams, in my darkest hour

Em7   D   C   D   Am7
    You are the Lord of all I am

        C   D
So won't You reign in me again?

INTERLUDE:

G D C G D C

VERSE 2:

G   D   C   D
    Over ev'ry thought, over ev'ry word

G   D   C   D
    May my life reflect the beauty of my Lord

Em7   D   C   D   Am7
    'Cause You mean more to me than any earthly thing

        C   D
So won't You reign in me again?

(REPEAT CHORUS 3X)

TAG:

Am7   C   D
    Won't You reign in me again?

OUTRO:

G D C G D C (hold)

WE WANT TO SEE JESUS LIFTED HIGH

DOUG HORLEY

Key of **G Major**, 4/4

INTRO (2X):

G D   Em   C

VERSE:

G   D
   We want to see Jesus lifted high
Em   C
   A banner that flies across this land
G   D
   That all men might see the truth and know
Em   C
   He is the way to heaven

(REPEAT VERSE)

CHORUS 1:

G   D
   We want to see,   we want to see
Em   C   G/B   Am7   G
   We want to see Je - sus   lift - ed high
G   D
   We want to see,   we want to see
Em   C   G/B   Am7   G
   We want to see Je - sus   lift - ed high

INTERLUDE:

G D   Em   C

(REPEAT VERSE & CHORUS 1)

BRIDGE:

        D   Em
Step by step, we're moving forward
        D   Em
Little by little, taking ground
        D   Em
Ev'ry prayer a pow'rful weapon
           C   D
Strongholds come tumbling down
   and down and down and down

(REPEAT VERSE & CHORUS 1)

CHORUS 2:

G   D
   We're gonna see,   we're gonna see
Em   C   G/B   Am7   G
   We're gonna see Je - sus   lift - ed high
G   D
   We're gonna see,   we're gonna see
Em   C   G/B   Am7   G
   We're gonna see Je - sus   lift - ed high

OUTRO: (Vocal ad lib.)

G D   Em   C

G   D   Em   C   G/B   Am7   G

WORTHY IS THE LAMB

DARLENE ZSCHECH

Key of **G Major, 4/4**

INTRO:

Em7   G   Em7   G

VERSE:

                C   G/B
Thank You for the cross, Lord

                C   D   G
Thank You for the price You paid

            D/E   Em7   D   C
Bearing all my sin and shame, in love You came

    Am7   G/B   D
And gave amazing grace

G   G/B   C   G/B
Thank You for this love, Lord

             C   D   G
Thank You for the nail-pierced hands

            D/E   Em7   D   C
Washed me in Your cleansing flow, now all I know:

    Am7   G/B   D
Your forgiveness and embrace

CHORUS:

G   D/F♯ Am7 G/B   C
Worthy is the Lamb, seated on the throne

D   D/C   G/B   C   Am7 C/G   D D/F♯
Crown You now with many crowns, You reign victorious

G   D/F♯ Am7 G/B   C
High and lifted up,   Jesus, Son of God

    D   D/C G/B C   Dsus
The Treasure of heaven crucified

        Am7 G/B   C
Worthy is the Lamb

        Am7 G/B Dsus
Worthy is the Lamb

(REPEAT VERSE)

(REPEAT CHORUS 2X)

TAG:

                  Am7 G/B C
Worthy is the Lamb

                  Am7 G/B Dsus
Worthy is the Lamb

                  G (hold)
Worthy is the Lamb